LOOKING AT THE
BIG PICTURE

HOLISTIC THINKING KIDS

BY: KRISTY HAMMILL

Published and written by Kristy Hammill

ISBN: 978-1-7751638-7-9

Copyright © 2019 by Kristy Hammill

www.holisticthinking.org

Dedicated to my brother
who always rides his bike.

I might be small in size,

but I have **BIG** ideas.

When I wake up in the morning, I open my curtains and let the bright sunshine fill my room. Who needs lightbulbs when we have the sun?

If everybody did that, just imagine how much less energy we would burn.

When I head downstairs for breakfast, I help mom make a healthy breakfast with lots of fruits and vegetables. This way I can stay healthy and strong.

If everybody did that, just imagine how much less sickness we would see.

When it's time to leave for school, I get out my bike and ride to school instead of dad driving me in the car.

If everybody did that, just imagine how much less gas fumes we would let into the air!

My bike was given to me by my neighbour. It was his brother's bike before that. If we take care of our stuff, then we can pass it down to others when we are finished with it.

If everybody did that, just imagine how much less junk we would have in our landfills.

In class, when I paint a picture, I always use both sides of the page so that I don't waste paper.

If everybody did that, just imagine how many trees we could save!

During math class, I helped Mr. Gray capture the bee that was buzzing around the room. We set it free outside instead of squishing him.

If everybody did that, just imagine how many more flowers we would have in the world, not to mention the strawberries!

I always pack home-made snacks in my lunch instead of bringing pre-packaged food. It's healthier and there is no garbage.

If everybody did that, just imagine how much less waste we would create!

When I notice that someone is standing all alone at the playground, I go and ask if they'd like to play with me.

If everybody did that, just imagine how much kindness we could spread in our world.

After school, my dad and I peel carrots and apples and cut them up for a snack. Then we compost the peels and leftover pieces to use in the garden next Spring.

If everybody did that, we would have lots of healthy dirt to grow new vegetables and a lot less garbage in the dump!

After our snack I head outside to play with my friends from next door instead of watching TV.

If everybody did that, just imagine how many friends would be outside to play with!

At dinner time I always say thanks for all the wonderful things that happened to me that day.

If everybody did that, just imagine how grateful and lucky everyone would feel.

At bedtime I always have a quick shower and wash up. I try not to stay in any longer than I need to.

If everybody did this, just imagine

how much water we would save!

If everybody tries to think about the big picture when they make decisions, then all of us little people can make a big difference!

Hello Readers!

I am an independent author and Amazon reviews can make a huge difference to the overall success for this book and of my Holistic Thinking Kids Series!

I personally read every single review that comes in, so if you enjoyed reading this book as much as I enjoyed writing it, please consider taking a few moments to leave a quick review. I would really appreciate it!

Thank you!

Kristy Hammill